HIR

≒ A PLAY ≒

TAYLOR MAC

NORTHWESTERN UNIVERSITY PRESS

EVANSTON, ILLINOIS

Northwestern University Press
www.nupress.northwestern.edu

Printed in the United States of America

10   9   8   7   6   5

ISBN 978-0-8101-3358-7 (paper)
ISBN 978-0-8101-3359-4 (e-book)

Library of Congress Cataloging-in-Publication data are available from the Library of Congress.

♾ The paper used in this publication meets the minimum requirements of the American National Standard for Information Sciences—Permanence of Paper for Printed Library Materials, ANSI Z39.48-1992.

CONTENTS

Acknowledgments *vii*

A Few Notes from the Playwright *ix*

Production History *xi*

Hir 1

ACKNOWLEDGMENTS

The author would like to thank the many people and institutions over the years who gave their feedback and time to the development of this play, specifically, Nina Mankin, Morgan Jenness, Leah Hamos, Tim Phillips, Josh Hecht, Lisa McNulty, Amy Kossow, Dale Soules, David Greenspan, Phyllis Somerville, Bianca Leigh, Stacey Karpen, Laryssa Husiak, Libby King, Kristen Sieh, Brian Hastert, Ashley Atkinson, Emily Morse, Kristin Nielsen, Larry Pine, Jax Jackson, Mark Anderson Phillips, Nancy Opel, Ben Euphrat, Quiara Alegrai Hudes, Lucas Hnath, Mia Chung, Dixon Place, New Dramatists, and especially Niegel Smith, Shirley Fischmen, the Magic Theatre, and the wonderful Loretta Greco.

A FEW NOTES FROM THE PLAYWRIGHT

ABSURD REALISM

I'm choosing to identify this play as "absurd realism." The absurdity comes from a heightened but realistic point of view. For example, the blinds are broken and nobody has bothered to fix them. This means that at a certain point during the day the sun shines into the house so brightly that everyone wears sunglasses or walks around with their hands shielding their eyes. Absurd realism is simply realistic characters in a realistic circumstance that is so extreme it is absurd. If at any moment it feels like your production is venturing into theater of the absurd, theater of the ridiculous, a Brechtian remove, or a metatheatrical deconstruction, then rein it in. Likewise, if it feels like realism is steering every choice, try to find the absurdity in that realism and turn the volume up.

ITALICS

The family calls Isaac *I*, as a nickname. It is italicized throughout so that it can be distinguished from the first person singular. Other italicized words indicate when a word is stressed. If you, as the actor or director, feel that a different emphasis is more natural and that the meaning isn't changed, then feel free to ignore the indicated emphases (but make sure you try them a few times first).

ARNOLD'S INTERJECTIONS

Many of Arnold's one-word interjections weren't intended to be given the full weight of a line. The director and actors must pick and choose.

The actor playing Arnold should feel free to improvise additional grunts and sounds throughout (as should all the actors), but not actual words.

MOTHER/MAMA

When Isaac calls Paige "Mother," he is scolding her. When he calls her "Mama," he's trying to get on her good side by playing her vulnerable boy.

ACTUAL CONCERN

For the most part Paige either takes the tough love approach with Isaac or tries to entertain him and be silly with him, as a way to avoid dealing with his pain. Perhaps five or six times in the play her concern for him loses the edge of frivolity. These are indicated in the stage directions when it says, "actual concern."

?

A question mark, where dialogue would be, indicates that the character gestures or expresses a nonverbal confusion. They take the time it would take to say, "What," "Duh," or "Okay?"

PRODUCTION HISTORY

The world premiere of *Hir* was on February 4, 2014, at Magic Theatre in San Francisco. Loretta Greco was the producing artistic director. The play was directed by Niegel Smith, with scenic design by Alexis Distler, costume design by Christine Crook, lighting design by Mike Inwood, sound design by Sara Huddleston, and dramaturgy by Shirley Fishman. The play, by Taylor Mac, was developed by the Magic Theatre and through the Creativity Fund, a program of New Dramatists.

Paige	Nancy Opel
Arnold	Mark Anderson Phillips
Isaac	Ben Euphrat
Max	Jax Jackson

The New York City premiere of *Hir* was in October 2015, presented by Playwrights Horizons, Inc. It was directed by Niegel Smith, with scenic design by David Zinn, costume design by Gabriel Berry, lighting design by Mike Inwood, and sound design by Fitz Patton. The cast was as follows:

Paige	Kristine Nielsen
Arnold	Daniel Oreskes
Isaac	Cameron Scoggins
Max	Tom Phelan

HIR

CHARACTERS

Paige Connor, 55. Cisgender mother to Max and Isaac. Wife to Arnold. Main actions are to entertain, excite (with new information she's discovered), and tear apart the old regimes.

Arnold Connor, 58. Cisgender father to Isaac and Max. Husband to Paige. Main actions are those of an old dog: eat, sleep, and get comfortable. Arnold was an angry man but has had a stroke, which turned him into more of a clown—rather like a slower and older Harpo Marx. When he feels something, he expresses it, uncensored. In a heartbeat, he can switch from complete joy to complete sorrow and back again.

Isaac Connor, 24. Cisgender son of Paige and Arnold. Brother to Max. Main actions are to assess the situation, assert himself, convert, and keep things under control. The action is, for Isaac, one long attempt at squashing down a major PTSD explosion. At times he is more successful than others (meaning he can almost relax) and he uses different, lighter tactics (including teasing), but ultimately he fails. There should be peaks and valleys, but a slow burn is what's been crafted into the play.

Max Connor, 17. Transgender child of Paige and Arnold. Sibling to Isaac. Main actions are to excite (with new information ze's discovered), ward off attacks, showboat, raise hir status on the family totem pole, and stake hir intellectual territory. Ideally, the actor playing Max should be someone who was a biological female and now identifies as transgender or gender-queer.

SETTING

The action of the play takes place in the kitchen and family room of a prairie-style house in the central valley of California, during a particularly hot summer, in August. It is the kind of home that, no matter how hard you clean, will always seem dirty. Dishes are piled up in the sink; the cracking wallpaper bears decade-old stains; piles of laundry are strewn about to the point where it's difficult to walk; and there seems to be a layer of dust on everything. It is an absolute disaster. There are two doors: the front door, and the back door, which leads to a medium-sized backyard. A hallway leads from the kitchen to the bedrooms. Arnold's cot is visible in the living room, as is part of the couch. The house was built by a first-time builder, in the early '70s, never intended to last as long as it has. It is a starter home that never really got started and can't seem to end.

ACT 1

[*Seven o'clock in the morning.* PAIGE *is waiting by the door, looking out of it. She's had too much coffee.* ARNOLD *eats a bowl of mush as someone with brain damage would. He wears a frilly woman's nightgown. He has extreme makeup on and a clown wig, making him look like an effeminate cross-dressing clown.* PAIGE *pours herself another cup of coffee. She goes back to the door.*]

ISAAC [*trying to open the front door, which is blocked by too much stuff*]: I'm home—

PAIGE: Honey?

ISAAC [*trying to open the door*]: Is something blocking the door?

PAIGE: Come around back. Arnold, get in your place!

ISAAC: Why won't the door open?

PAIGE: I thought you'd use the back.

ISAAC: Why wouldn't I use the front door?

PAIGE: It's blocked.

ISAAC: What's blocking it?

PAIGE: We were getting rid of things and stopped caring.

ISAAC: So you left stuff blocking the door?

PAIGE: Come around back.

ISAAC: You can't move the stuff?

PAIGE: There's too much.

ISAAC: That's a fire hazard, Mom.

PAIGE: Oh, wouldn't that be wonderful.

ISAAC: What?

PAIGE: Come around back.

ISAAC: I'm coming 'round back.

PAIGE: What?

ISAAC: I said—

PAIGE: Come around back.

ISAAC: I know.

PAIGE [*running to the hallway and shouting down it*]: MAAAAAAAAX, YOUR BROTHER IS FINALLY HERE FROM THE WAR!

[*To* ARNOLD, *excited for* ISAAC *to see* ARNOLD *in his place, dressed like a clown*] Arnie. Away from the door. Arnie. Arnie away from the door. Arnie. Arnold, sit in your chair. Your chair. Sit in your chair. Arnold! Get in your place for *I*.

[PAIGE *loses patience and moves* ARNOLD *to the chair*.]

ISAAC [*opening the back door and entering*]: Why's the lawn so overgrown—

[*Seeing the disaster that is the home*] OOAH!

PAIGE [*scared by* ISAAC's *scream*]: OOAH!

ISAAC: JESUS HELL!

PAIGE [*laughing*]: You scared me.

ISAAC: What happened?

PAIGE: Why did you yell like that?

ISAAC: It's a fucking disaster in here.

PAIGE: Language.

ISAAC: What—

PAIGE [*to* ISAAC]: Sit down.

ISAAC [*meaning, "answer me"*]: Mom!

PAIGE [*excited to tell him*]: Honey, sit down, I have so much to tell you. Arnie, close the door.

ISAAC [*seeing* ARNOLD *for the first time and freaking out*]: OOAH!

PAIGE [*another scared scream at his scream*]: OOAH!

[*Laughing*] You keep scaring me.

ISAAC: DAD?

PAIGE [*to* ISAAC]: Isn't it great. Arnie, close the door, you can see the heat in waves. Arnie, close the door. The air can't fight the world. We're cooling and heating the planet at the same time. Arnie, close the door. Arnie, close the door. The door. Close it. Close it. Close the door. Yes the door. Yes the door, the door. Close the door.

ISAAC: I got it—

PAIGE [*to* ISAAC]: He will do it!

[*To* ARNOLD]: Arnie, close the door. Close the door. Arnold, close the door. Yes. The door. The door. Close the door. Close it. Close.

Close. Close the door. Close the door. Close the door, close the door, close the door, close the door, close the door. Door. Door. Door. Close. Close door. Yes. Hand. Hand on knob. Hand on knob. Yes. Yes. Push. Push. Yes. YES. CLOSE THE DOOR!

[ARNOLD *closes the door. Pause.* ISAAC *suddenly runs to the kitchen sink and pukes.* PAIGE *almost goes to help him but doesn't know what to do.*]

ISAAC: Why are there dishes everywhere?

ARNOLD [*going to turn the air-conditioning off*]: It's cold.

PAIGE: Don't you turn off that air.

ISAAC [*to* ARNOLD]: Why are you dressed like that?

ARNOLD: It's cold.

PAIGE [*calling down the hallway to* MAX]: MAAAAAAAAX. GET IN HERE. YOUR BROTHER HAS FINALLY ARRIVED AND I WOULD RATHER NOT BE ANY LATER THAN WE'RE ALREADY GOING TO BE.

ARNOLD [*holding his penis, which is a habit he has*]: It's cold.

PAIGE: Yes, we heard you, Arnie.

ISAAC: Why is there air-conditioning?

PAIGE: I wanted it.

ISAAC: He's shivering.

PAIGE: Of course he is. It's freezing in here.

ISAAC [*going to turn the air-conditioning off*]: He hates air-conditioning.

PAIGE: Don't you touch that air. That air goes off when I say it goes off.

[*Excited to share this new information*] This is not a house of sweat anymore, Isaac.

[*To* ARNOLD, *while throwing him a pink sweater with bedazzled kittens embroidered on it and reprimanding him for not following the rules*] You *know* when you're cold, you put on Sparkle Kitty.

ARNOLD: Sparkle.

PAIGE: Don't hold your penis.

ARNOLD: Penis.

[PAIGE *squirts* ARNOLD *with a spray bottle, the way you would a cat you're trying to train.*]

ISAAC: Dad, why do you have makeup on?

PAIGE [*a realization*]: I forgot his estrogen. Too much new stuff. His complacence is contingent on the routines.

[*As if to say, "How could anyone keep track of all this?"*] Look at his pills. There's all kinds of rules about when and how but I figure, if he doesn't have that long to live, all at once is fine. He won't swallow them so you have to put them in a shaky-shake. It takes him forever to drink it so you have to sit with him.

[*During the following she makes* ARNOLD *his shake.*]

ISAAC: The doctors prescribed him estrogen?

PAIGE: Oh god no. The doctors prescribed him poodle-diddle-wing-wang. The estrogen's extra.

ISAAC: ?

PAIGE: It keeps him docile.

ISAAC: He's gonna grow tits.

PAIGE [*commenting on his speech*]: Grammar!

ISAAC: He's *going* to grow tits.

PAIGE: Language!

ISAAC: He's going to grow breasts.

PAIGE: Then he can fondle *himself.*

> [*Actually concerned about* ISAAC] You're so skinny. Isn't the military suppose to make you bulky?

ISAAC: You can't give him, Dad . . . men, estrogen.

PAIGE: Is that what the Marine Medical Affairs says?

ISAAC: I'm in the Mortuary Affairs. It's not medical. I pick up guts. Exploded guts.

PAIGE [*suddenly emotional, regarding how dangerous* ISAAC's *job is*]: Whose fault is that, that you chose to join the *Mortuary* Affairs?

ISAAC: Someone has to do it.

PAIGE: Someone does not have to do it.

ISAAC: You can't leave body parts lying around.

PAIGE: If it means *you* risking your life to pick them up, yes, you can.

ISAAC: The families need me to send their kids home.

PAIGE: You read that in the handbook.

ISAAC: That doesn't make it untrue.

PAIGE [*actual concern*]: You don't know what that job has done to you, *I.*

ISAAC: I'm okay.

PAIGE [*actual concern*]: You don't know what you are. These things sneak up on you. They infect.

ISAAC: Nothing's wrong with me.

PAIGE: You think that because you've gotten numb to it. You can't pick up dead things every day and not get numb to it.

ISAAC: I'm fine.

PAIGE: You're obviously not fine.

ISAAC: Why does he have makeup on?

PAIGE: We were supposed to start this off right. [*Slight pause*] It's just makeup.

ISAAC: He put makeup on himself?

PAIGE: I was sitting around waiting for you.

ISAAC: You *made* him look like that?

PAIGE: It's what we do now. We play dress up. I thought it'd make you laugh.

ISAAC: Well it doesn't make me laugh. Fucking hell—

PAIGE: LANGUAGE!

ISAAC [*taking the wig off* ARNOLD *but speaking about* PAIGE]: What's the matter with you!

PAIGE: Oh don't do that. You'll spoil it.

ISAAC [*looking in a drawer where the rags used to be and not finding them*]: He let you do that to him?

PAIGE: He's not all there, *I*. It's okay. He doesn't even know.

ARNOLD: Err.

ISAAC [*looking through the laundry on the floor*]: I need a rag.

PAIGE: What for?

ISAAC: There's laundry everywhere!

PAIGE: I didn't want to fold it.

ISAAC: You left clean laundry on the floor?

PAIGE: I don't do laundry anymore.

ISAAC: It looks like a fucking squat in here. I can't find a rag. I need a rag. Why aren't they where they're supposed to be?

PAIGE: Use a shirt.

ISAAC: I NEED A RAG.

PAIGE [*throwing a T-shirt at him*]: USE A SHIRT. IT DOESN'T MATTER!

[ISAAC *tries to take* ARNOLD's *makeup off with the T-shirt.*]

[*Disappointed that he's taking* ARNOLD's *makeup off*] What? No. It took me all morning to do that face.

ARNOLD [*a little hurt by* ISAAC's *rough wiping*]: Err.

ISAAC: Sorry.

[ISAAC *goes to get some Crisco.*]

Where's the Crisco?

PAIGE: You want to make a stir-fry?

ISAAC: To take that shit off his face.

PAIGE: Isaac, slow down.

ISAAC [*regarding the Crisco*]: Why isn't it in its place?

PAIGE [*excited to share this new information*]: We don't *do* places anymore.

ISAAC [*opening a cupboard*]: You just put things in random cupboards?

[*The cupboard has nothing in it.*]

PAIGE: We don't do cupboards anymore. We don't do order. Places and cupboards are what your father wanted so now they're your father's job. And since he just likes to stand by the door hoping to flee, the house is a disaster.

[*During the following,* ARNOLD *gets up and stands by the door.*]

ARNOLD: Door.

PAIGE: He likes to escape and waddle through the neighborhood tract yards of mediocrity. You have to keep an eye on him. We're becoming the talk of the block. People *wave* at us. They never used to wave. Now they wave. They don't say hi. Just wave. Arnie, away from the door.

[*Calling down the hallway to* MAX] MAAAAAAX. WE WILL BE STUCK IN TRAFFIC.

ISAAC: I just got here. You're going somewhere?

PAIGE: You're coming with us. Saturdays are homeschool cultural outing days. We drive to the city and go to museums and galleries, concerts.

ISAAC: Homeschool?

PAIGE: The public school was not a healthy environment for Max.

ISAAC: You had one semester of junior college.

PAIGE: So?

ISAAC: You don't know enough to homeschool.

PAIGE: Don't you tell me what I know enough to do! [*Meaning, "if they are allowed to, I should be allowed to"*] People who believe Adam and Eve populated the planet are allowed to homeschool.

ISAAC: Everybody has problems at school. Problems are normal.

PAIGE: They let people homeschool who aren't sophisticated enough to understand metaphor.

ISAAC: If you needed help you should have told me, but you can't just take Max out of school.

PAIGE: I'm all about the metaphor now.

ISAAC: She's the smart one. You're gonna ruin that.

PAIGE: Don't you tell me what I am and am not qualified to do.

ISAAC: You can't do stuff like that. You can't dress people up in clown outfits and let the house go to seed. You said Dad had a *little* stroke but that he was okay. Look at him. That is not okay. WHAT IS HAPPENING!?!

PAIGE [*slight pause*]: You're not supposed to tell people who go to the wars about local adversity. Lots of things have happened, *I*, that we haven't told you. A refugee woman down the street got hit by a car. Should I have sent a tweet? She was running after her dog.

[*During the following* PAIGE *turns on the blender.* ISAAC *tries to keep it together as the noise gives him a little PTSD reaction.*]

[*Speaking loudly over the sound of the blender*] SHE CAME HERE TO ESCAPE BIG THINGS. SHE EXPECTED TO BE BLOWN UP, MUTILATED, OR EATEN BY A STOMACH WORM, BUT TO BE HIT BY A CAR? RUNNING AFTER HER DOG IN THE GOOD OLD U.S. OF A.? AFTER ALL THAT MISERY, YOU'D THINK SHE'D LEARN TO PRIORITIZE HERSELF OVER HER SCHNAUZER.

[ISAAC *pukes in the sink.*]

   [*Turning off the blender and with actual concern*] What's wrong?

ISAAC [*his head in the sink*]: I'm fine.

[PAIGE *turns on the blender.* ISAAC *starts puking.* PAIGE *turns off the blender.*]

PAIGE: Is it the blender?

ISAAC: No.

[PAIGE *turns on the blender.* ISAAC *starts to puke again.* PAIGE *turns off the blender.*]

PAIGE: I think it's the blender.

ISAAC: I'm fine.

[PAIGE *turns the blender on.* ISAAC *starts puking and* PAIGE *turns the blender off.* ISAAC *stops puking. Slight pause. She turns it on and* ISAAC *starts puking. She turns it off. He stops. On: puke. Off: no puke. On: puke. Off: no puke. Pause. On:* ISAAC *yanks the blender out of the socket. A pause.* PAIGE *puts her hand on his head. He shakes her off. Pause.*]

PAIGE: Are you going to apologize for being late?

ISAAC: Said seven.

PAIGE [*correcting* ISAAC*'s speech*]: *Who* said seven?

ISAAC: *You* said get here by seven. I'm here. It's seven.

PAIGE: I said I wanted to be on the road by seven.

ISAAC: Some people get parades and banners and I come home to this?

PAIGE [*a sincere question*]: You wanted a banner?

ISAAC: Yes. Three years away from home, in a war zone, I want to have a banner and cookies and a clean home and a father who isn't dressed up like some crazy tranny clown.

PAIGE: Don't say that word.

ISAAC: Clown?

PAIGE: Tranny. [*Obviously quoting someone*] "Only people who want to be reality TV stars say that word." [*Showing two sets of shoes*] How are the shoes?

ISAAC: Fine.

PAIGE: You can't let me know which ones you prefer?

ISAAC: They're both fine.

PAIGE: Yes, but who ever wanted to be fine? Whoever wanted to be a C student? [*Excited to share this new information*] You become a C student and you live a C life, Isaac.

ISAAC: The black ones.

PAIGE: Thank you.

[*She's about to put on the black shoes but then considers it might be sabotage and puts the light blue ones on to show him.*]

What's the situation?

ISAAC: You look . . . fine.

[*Slight pause.*]

PAIGE [*calling down the hallway*]: MAAAAAAX! WE ARE LEAVING IN TWO MINUTES.

ISAAC: Dad can't leave the house like that.

PAIGE [*surprised that* ISAAC *would think she'd take* ARNOLD]: He's not going. I've become a little more eccentric since last you saw me but I'm not insane.

ISAAC: Who's gonna take care of him?

PAIGE: *Gonna? Gonna!*

ISAAC: Who is going to look after him while we are supposed to be gone?

PAIGE: Nobody. Same as when we go to work. Plop him on the couch, lock the door, and he's there when we get back.

ISAAC: You leave him alone?

PAIGE: Yes.

ISAAC: All day.

PAIGE: I'm doing things. I'm not missing being part of the world to hang out with your father.

ISAAC: Dad *is* part of the world.

PAIGE [*as if smelling rotten milk*]: Ew.

ISAAC: Mother—

PAIGE [*slight pause*]: I discovered the most amazing thing, I. It used to be you could be a mediocre straight white man and be guaranteed a certain amount of success. But now you actually have to improve yourself. Because now . . . [*in a mock horror movie trailer voice-over voice*] The darkies have come. And the spics. And the queers. And those backstabbing bitches waiting to get at the mediocre straight white man the minute it becomes known he is barely lifting a finger but thinking he is lifting the world.

[*Back to her normal voice*] And when you left us, and I'm not blaming you for that— [*kind of blaming him*] God knows I'm not blaming you for leaving—

ISAAC: We couldn't afford college and I couldn't get a job.

PAIGE: But when you left us, it got much worse. Your father, furious over his waning privilege, also lost a third of his family to take his fury out on. But it had to go somewhere, right? It was frothing up inside of him. He started to get a constant white saliva stuck to the corners of his mouth. Pieces of his vitriol would spray all over his customers, who started calling in complaints about the racist plumber with the saliva who was sent to them by their trusted Roto-Rooter. He lost his job, *I*. He lost his job of thirty-three years to a Chinese American woman. A plumber who is a Chinese American *woman*. It was fantastic. But bereft of you and his customers to spray his red-faced spittle on, he doubled down on Max and me. Three times I had to take Max to the emergency room. Three times, Isaac. But, the incredible thing is, little tomboy Maxine wouldn't let her father stop her trajectory, so she gets herself some testosterone on the World Wide Web and starts to enlarge her clitoris.

ISAAC [*an exclamation as if to say, "What the fuck?"*]: OH!

PAIGE: You don't like that word, "clitoris"?

ISAAC: OH!

PAIGE: I didn't used to like it either. But now I love it. It's a great word. Clitoris.

ISAAC: Stop that.

PAIGE [*sung*]: Clitoris!

ISAAC: AHHHHH—

PAIGE: Don't be like your father. That's the kind of word that sent him over the edge. That *and* that his wife, seeing agency in her child, seeing Max change . . . After years of mollifying my own strength in fear of [*indicating* ARNOLD] him, I started to change myself. I got myself a JOB! Working at a NOT-FOR-PROFIT! "That fucking whore." That's what he called me for abandoning him to his jobless private sector. He couldn't handle the pressure of actually having to change to keep up, so about a year ago, blood decided it wouldn't go to his brain and he had a little stroke.

ISAAC: He's been this way for a year?

PAIGE: So?

ISAAC: On the phone you acted like it just happened.

PAIGE: You re-up twice and then don't talk to us for a *year* and *I'm* the unreasonable one?

ISAAC: I was in a fucking war zone.

PAIGE: LANGUAGE!

ISAAC [*looking at* ARNOLD *with something like pity*]: You should have told me.

PAIGE: Don't you pity him. Those who knew him, know of his cruelty, we will *not* rewrite his history with pity.

[*A pause as* PAIGE *stares at* ISAAC.]

I should show you your bed.

ISAAC: I remember where my—

PAIGE: Things change.

ISAAC: Clearly.

PAIGE: Max's old room is my craft room, your old room is now Max's, but Monsieur Couch will be happy to have you home.

ISAAC: You can't just . . . it's my room. I've been dreaming about sleeping in my room.

PAIGE: Well, adjust. Max was *enlarging,* and needed more space. [*Excited to share this information*] Ze is becoming an innovator in gender.

ISAAC: ?

PAIGE: Your sister is not your sister.

ISAAC: ?

PAIGE: Ze has become the new. A revolutionary.

ISAAC: TALK PLAINLY!

PAIGE: Isn't your generation supposed to be quick about these sorts of things?

ISAAC: Max is a . . .

PAIGE [*sung*]: *Transsexual.*

[ISAAC *rushes to the sink and pukes.*]

[*Calling down the hallway*] MAAAAAAAAX!

MAX [*calling from hir bedroom*]: I'M TAKING MY SHOT!

PAIGE: Oh god.

[*Calling down the hallway*] HONEY, WE'LL BE IN A CAR FOR THREE HOURS, MAYBE NOW IS NOT THE BEST TIME TO PUMP YOURSELF UP.

[*To* ISAAC] Max is on the mones.

ISAAC: Moans?

PAIGE: Hormones. That's what they call them. Your mother is hip. She knows the lingo. Don't they teach you anything in the Marines?

ISAAC: She is a he?

PAIGE: I credit the Cheetos. How could we feed our children fluorescent food and not expect a little gender confluence? You have a brother now. No! Not a brother. You have a *something*.

[*Calling down the hallway*] MAAAAAAAAX COME IN HERE AND EXPLAIN YOUR AMBIGUITY TO YOUR BROTHER.

[*To* ISAAC] Isaac, stay with me. What you think you know, you do not know. There are no longer two genders. No longer simply a Y and X chromosome but an alphabet of genders. They call it the LGBTTSQQIAA community. Or what I call the gender of [*pronouncing LGBTTSQQIAA as if it were a word*] Lugabuttsqueeah.

ARNOLD: Lugabuttsqueeah.

PAIGE: In these new genders, exist new pronouns. Max is no longer a she or a he. So you call Max "ze." You must use "ze" instead of the pronouns "he" or "she" and you must use the pronoun [*pronounced "here"*] "hir," H.I.R., in place of the pronouns "her" or "him." Max gets very upset if you refer to hir as a she, he, her, or him. Ze wants you to refer to hir as a hir or ze. Ze also gets upset when you emphasize the "ze" as if commenting on the pronoun when speaking to hir. For example if you were to say, "What is ZE doing today?" ze will not like that. Ze, understandably, is not to be treated as a sideshow oddity. Ze wants you to say "ze" or "hir" as if this had been part of your regular speaking vocabulary your entire life. Any breach in decorum will cause hir to write in hir blog about how awful hir troglodyte fascist heteronormative mother is. It's fantastic.

ISAAC: I'm confused.

ARNOLD: Lugabuttsqueeah.

PAIGE: Max is the root of who we are. Truly. The root of who we are and the cusp of the new. There has never been any such thing as men and women and, Isaac, there never will be. You know all those pretty fish in coral reefs? They're transgender. It's true. I looked it up. When Max was getting beat up in school, then coming home for more, from your father, I didn't know what to do. They kept saying, "It gets better!", but it didn't seem like it was going to get better, so I started search-engine-ing. I started to learn things. It was like being baptized, only without the male-dominated hegemonic paradigm. Everyone is a little bit of everything, Isaac. We're simply us. Hir. [*Gesturing to the house disdainfully*] Not here. [*Feeling all around her body parts, sensually, and then throwing her arms out and up, as if to say her body is all genders and it must be shot out into the universe*] But HIR.

ISAAC: Stop.

PAIGE: All this fog over my eyes for so many years. And it simply lifted. Once I learned one thing, I could learn another. And pretty soon I could start coming up with my own theories, or at least theories I hadn't heard from other people first. This is my theory. We all come from fish. My whole life I'm told I was made out of a rib. What did your father call me?

ISAAC: Rib.

PAIGE: "Hey Rib, get me a beer." That's what that man would say to your mother.

ARNOLD: Rib.

[PAIGE *sprays* ARNOLD *with the spray bottle.*]

PAIGE [*blaming him a little*]: I'm not blaming you, I, for standing by while he called me that. You were the child and I was the adult. I let you be raised in a way that would allow you to stand by. But I wasn't a rib. In actuality I was, we were all, TRANSGENDER FISH. Which means that part of me, despite the years of clamping down into one single homogeneous gender, is still multifaceted. *And* we're all from Africa. So that means we're all black. *And* we all masturbate, so that means we're all a little gay. You're GAY, Isaac.

ISAAC [*he is not gay*]: I'm not gay.

PAIGE: You are. Just a little. And so am I and so is Max. We're all everything. And it took Max's being born a little more blatantly that way than the rest of us for me to figure it out. Max saved me. I didn't have to be beat up by your father. I was bigger than that. I was a father. And a mother. I *am* a father. And a mother. We are all hir. [*Gesturing to the house*] Not here. [*Touching all over her body, sensually, and shooting it out and up again*] But HIR!

ISAAC: Stop that!

PAIGE [*calling down the hallway*]: MAAAAAAX, COME SAY HEL—

MAX [*entering, wearing a "wife-beater" tank top*]: ALL RIGHT! STOP NAGGING, I'M COMING!

[*A pause as* ISAAC *looks at* MAX. ISAAC *runs to the sink and throws up in it.*]

THAT'S NOT OKAY!

[*To* PAIGE, *as if* ISAAC *weren't present*] He picks up decapitated heads for a living and when he sees me, he pukes?

[*To* ISAAC] THAT IS SO NOT OKAY!

[*The next six lines are a private conversation, as if* ISAAC *weren't present.*]

PAIGE: It's not because he saw you.

MAX: Of course it is.

PAIGE: He pukes because of the blender.

MAX: That doesn't make sense.

PAIGE [*going to plug the blender in*]: Watch.

[ISAAC *grabs the blender and pulls it away from her.*]

MAX: He got sick when he saw me. You always try to say things aren't
   because of me but they're always because of me.

ISAAC: You have a beard.

MAX: Fuck you.

PAIGE: LANGUAGE.

[*As a way of getting out hir aggression,* MAX *shows off hir muscles,
which are relatively small, in a crab pose.*]

MAX [*a frustrated outburst*]: Yaahr!

PAIGE [*to* MAX]: Just because you have muscles doesn't mean you get
   to be tacky.

ISAAC: She has a beard.

MAX: ZE! You say "ze" for he or she and "hir" for her or him.

PAIGE [*to* ISAAC]: Just say *Max.* That's what I did at first. Until I got
   used to the pronoun.

MAX: It's not that hard.

PAIGE: The youth don't understand you can't mess with content and
   form at the same time.

MAX [*a passive-aggressive attack*]: You're smaller.

ISAAC: What?

MAX: I thought you were supposed to get big in the military but you got smaller.

ISAAC: You have a beard.

MAX: Kinda.

PAIGE [*encouraging*]: It'll grow in more.

ISAAC: You don't not prep a person for that. Send a picture or something.

MAX: I have a dick too. Should I send a picture of that?

PAIGE: You *have* an enlarged clitoris.

MAX [*to* PAIGE, *accusing*]: Could we not talk about my genitalia!

PAIGE: You started it.

[ISAAC *pukes.*]

MAX [*a demand*]: Give me a hug!

[ISAAC *pukes again.*]

Tell him to give me a hug.

PAIGE: *I,* stop puking and give Max a hug.

MAX: Do it!

[ISAAC *wipes his face and hugs* MAX. *It is a genuine hug that lasts during the following dialogue.*]

PAIGE: Now this is how I wanted it.

[*To the universe*] Thank you.

ISAAC: You don't smell like you.

MAX: I know, it's cool.

ISAAC: Why don't you smell like you?

PAIGE: Be nice.

ISAAC: And you're clammy.

MAX: I'm nervous.

ISAAC: Why?

MAX [*pushing* ISAAC *away, while reverting to being the bratty younger sibling, and getting back at* ISAAC *for not being sensitive to hir needs*]: Shouldn't you be in orange?

ISAAC: What?

MAX: Shouldn't you be wearing some orange jumpsuit?

ISAAC: I'm not a convict. I didn't get arrested.

PAIGE [*sarcasm*]: Thank god for you.

ISAAC: You could be a little nicer.

PAIGE: I keep forgetting we're not treating our dishonorably discharged addicts with disdain.

ISAAC: I'm not an addict.

PAIGE [*an accusation*]: Please.

ISAAC [*a bad liar*]: I was experimenting.

PAIGE: People say they're experimenting so they don't have to admit they're wrong.

MAX: I told you that.

PAIGE [*to* ISAAC]: Now you can actually major in Experimenting. At the university. With a minor in Weighing Your Options.

MAX: That's my line. I told you that and you're acting like you made it up.

PAIGE: I give you credit.

MAX: You didn't.

PAIGE: Well give me time.

MAX: You wouldn't even know you can major in Experimentation if I hadn't shown you it in the catalog.

PAIGE: Footnote Max.

[*Speaking to the room at large as if there were hordes of listeners*] Everyone. Footnote Max.

ISAAC: You're going to college?

MAX: Hell no.

ARNOLD: College.

PAIGE [*spraying* ARNOLD]: We used to think college was the Holy Grail but now we know academia is where people go who are too afraid to have uninstitutionalized discourse.

MAX: Paige.

PAIGE: Footnote Max.

MAX: Why should you pay to learn when you can do it for free?

ISAAC: For a degree.

PAIGE: Eww.

MAX: I'm not getting in debt to experiment. People used to experiment to figure things out but now they've turned experimenting into a craft. Academia is a Ponzi scheme.

PAIGE [*getting back at* MAX]: *You* didn't say *that*, who said *that*?

MAX [*admitting ze didn't come up with this*]: Sarah Schulman.

PAIGE: Who's that?

MAX: We read her book.

PAIGE: We did?

MAX: *The Gentrification of the Mind.*

PAIGE: Right.

MAX: You didn't read it?

PAIGE: I did.

MAX: What was it about?

PAIGE: How the mind can be gentrified.

MAX: You don't know ANYTHING!

PAIGE: You're being mean.

MAX: I am emancipating and leaving.

PAIGE: I know, and I encourage you.

MAX [*to* PAIGE]: When I turn eighteen, I'm going to live on a Radical Faerie commune.

PAIGE: With your mother.

MAX [*to* PAIGE, *an attack regarding everything they don't do*]: A Radical Faerie commune where they have gender queers who have actual discourse and ideas and where they grow their own food and recycle and have heart circles and sexual freedom and where nobody yells at each other.

PAIGE: Now you're being cruel.

ISAAC: I just got here. You're leaving?

MAX: Are you planning on sticking around?

ISAAC: Yes. Someone obviously needs to be here.

PAIGE: We're doing great.

ISAAC [*regarding* ARNOLD]: *He* is not doing great. This house is not doing great.

PAIGE: You want to take charge but you can't even arrive on time.

ISAAC: You could have picked me up but you didn't and so I had to walk from the bus station over all the downtown homeless vets. Thank you for that.

PAIGE: I didn't pick you up because I wanted you to see all those vets, shooting up.

ISAAC: I didn't shoot up.

MAX: He snorted it.

PAIGE [*sarcastic*]: Well, what a relief. Just snorting?

ISAAC: Yes!

PAIGE: Up your nose?

ISAAC: Yes.

MAX: We heard differently.

ISAAC: Jesus Christ.

PAIGE: You think I get an official notice saying you've been dishonorably discharged and I sit around waiting to get the details? I research.

MAX [*meaning ze did all the work*]: I research.

PAIGE: I made the phone calls, *you* found them on the intercom.

MAX: Internet.

PAIGE: I know the proper name, Max. The more your beard grows in, the more literal you get. The point is, [*back to* ISAAC] I heard differently.

ISAAC: Not just the nose then.

PAIGE: Where?

ISAAC: You obviously know.

PAIGE: I don't.

ISAAC: You just said you know. Why make me tell you?

PAIGE: It is all so unbelievable, I would like some confirmation.

[*A standoff.*]

ISAAC [*quietly*]: My butt.

PAIGE: What?

MAX: His butt.

PAIGE: I heard him. I want him to say it again.

ISAAC: My butt.

PAIGE: Your what?

ARNOLD: Butt.

ISAAC: My ASSHOLE! I got caught blowing crystal meth up my ASSHOLE!

PAIGE [*shaming him*]: Up! Your asshole!

ISAAC: Yes.

PAIGE: How does that work exactly?

ISAAC: ?

PAIGE [*a genuine question*]: How does one blow an illegal substance up an asshole?

MAX: With a straw.

PAIGE [*a great discovery*]: With a straw!

ISAAC: Yes.

[PAIGE *takes a bendy-straw from the kitchen and attempts to figure out how she would blow crystal up her butt with it. This goes on for a bit before* ISAAC *interrupts it.*]

A girl blew it in there for me.

PAIGE: It was a team effort?

ISAAC: Yes, generally it is a team effort.

PAIGE: An Afghani girl or a soldier girl?

ISAAC: Does it matter?

MAX: Was she hot?

PAIGE [*a reprimand*]: Ew!

ARNOLD: Hot.

PAIGE [*spraying* ARNOLD *but talking to* MAX]: What was that? You don't talk like that?

MAX: I was just wondering.

PAIGE [*back to* ISAAC]: The questions are: Are you exploring the local culture? Hiring this girl? Or seducing a member of the military with the titillating promise of blowing drugs through a straw up your asshole?

ISAAC: I don't have to tell you that.

PAIGE: I want to know how far down I'm supposed to go before I can start dragging you back with me.

ISAAC: I am an adult and a Marine and I don't have to tell you things I don't want to.

PAIGE: Isaac, how are you going to be part of this new world we're going to if you don't face how your choices aren't working for you.

ISAAC: I just survived a war. Things are working.

PAIGE: You just puked two kidneys and a crack den into that sink.

ISAAC: I'll be fine.

[*The following, until* ISAAC *speaks, is a conversation as if* ISAAC *weren't in the room listening.*]

MAX: Meth doesn't make you puke.

PAIGE: I know.

MAX: We researched this.

PAIGE: I know.

MAX: And it's not crack. It's meth.

PAIGE: I *know,* honey, I just said he puked a crack den because it was my way of redirecting his PTSD.

ISAAC: I don't have PTSD, I just need my home to be my home. Jesus Christ!

PAIGE: Don't you get biblical on me. [*Still not having gotten over the insult from earlier*] People who believe in Noah and the Ark are allowed to homeschool.

MAX: That story's transphobic.

PAIGE AND ISAAC: What?

MAX: Noah and the Ark. It's transphobic.

PAIGE [*wanting to learn*]: What do you mean?

MAX: One of each gender of animal?

PAIGE: Oh.

ISAAC: Oh come on!

MAX: Did Noah invite the African dog that starts off as a male and turns into a female later in life?

PAIGE: I don't know.

MAX: I don't think he did.

PAIGE: You're shifting my paradigm, Max. See, Isaac.

MAX: Did he invite the snakes that don't care about their gender and procreate by having massive snake orgies?

PAIGE: Really?

MAX: Or the squids at the bottom of the ocean, where it's so dark they don't know who they're having sex with, they just—[*squirting the spray bottle*] squirt their sperm all over.

PAIGE [*scolding*]: Okay, that's graphic.

MAX: No, he left those squid out of the story.

ISAAC: Because they were squid and didn't need to be on a boat.

PAIGE: That's a good point.

MAX: The *point* being the story completely ignores that there are more than two genders in the world. There's a whole alphabet of genders—

PAIGE: I told him that part.

MAX: Oh.

PAIGE: I'm sorry. Did you want to tell him? I'm sorry, baby.

MAX [*it obviously matters*]: It doesn't matter.

PAIGE: You see Isaac, Max is learning things even though we're homeschooling. Things are truly good now. Your father's out of the picture and it's not like how it was before.

ARNOLD: Picture.

PAIGE [*a dirty secret*]: I have employees. Your mother has employees.

MAX [*meaning, "I'm her only employee"*]: You have one employee. Me.

PAIGE: Max is my intern.

MAX: Forced unpaid laborer.

ISAAC [*some judgment on it being a not-for-profit*]: At the not-for-profit.

PAIGE: It's called Rural Sprawl, kind of like urban sprawl.

MAX [*meaning, "Mom is so stupid to like this name"*]: But the opposite.

PAIGE: We're working to get rid of the landfill so we can make this area farmland again.

ISAAC: We live on the landfill. You can't get rid of the landfill. There's a whole neighborhood built on top of the landfill.

PAIGE: I know, *I*, but housing capacity is down and so much of this *suburban* sprawl's just hanging out empty—

MAX: And most everybody is happy to sell cheap and get out.

PAIGE: So Rural Sprawl is buying up the property.

MAX: We want to make it safe space.

PAIGE: But we're not just stopping there, because people used to make pockets of safe space but our goal is to make the whole world safe space, right honey?

MAX [*a little funny that Mom is so into this*]: Right.

PAIGE: I have a title now. I'm the Community Coordinator.

MAX [*belittling* PAIGE]: She's like a land trust Avon Lady.

PAIGE: Are you belittling me?

MAX: Just saying—

PAIGE: I don't like that. Don't do that please.

MAX: You put on lipstick and panty hose, go from door to door, hand out brochures, and barely make any money selling people the idea of freedom.

PAIGE: Yes.

MAX: Just like Avon.

PAIGE: I understand you don't have the historical context, maturity, or estrogen to comprehend the sexism of your statement, but all the same I'd appreciate it if you would refrain from equating my work with something you deem frivolous.

MAX [*a sincere apology*]: Sorry.

ISAAC: We *need* this neighborhood. Our home is in this neighborhood.

PAIGE: I know, but this is our way out of it.

ISAAC: We were raised here.

MAX: Home is a mechanism of control.

PAIGE [*sung*]: Paradigm shift!

ISAAC: Dad built this house.

PAIGE: Cheap plywood and glue.

ISAAC: We *make* the home so *we* are the ones who *control* the home.

PAIGE: Tell that to all the neighbors who have had to get three jobs, never see their kids, and still can't make ends meet, all so they can keep their Formica countertops.

ISAAC: You can't think straight because this place is a disaster. We have to get this all back on track.

PAIGE: A person can only dust collectible plates from Reno for so long before said person goes a little batty. Do you follow me? I've gone a little batty. But not so much that I'd lift another finger to clean one speck of this goddamn starter home we've been in for thirty years.

[ISAAC *picks up a cardboard box that is lying open on its side.*]

ARNOLD: Ah!

[ISAAC *dumps out the contents of the box and starts putting laundry in it.*]

PAIGE: What are you doing? Don't do that.

ISAAC: I'm finding the floor so I can walk on it.

PAIGE: That's your father's bed.

ISAAC: The laundry?

MAX: The box.

PAIGE [*a defense*]: He prefers it.

MAX: It's his little hut.

ISAAC: We are not going to act like the homeless in our own home.

MAX: It's not a home, it's a *starter* home.

ISAAC: Key word, *home*.

MAX: They're not the same thing.

PAIGE [*to* MAX]: Yes, work through that thought, honey?

MAX: Don't tell me what to work through. Dad built the house so that one day we could get a better house. And we only kept the house orderly so it would be ready to sell. And the harder he tried to sell it, but couldn't, the angrier he got, and the angrier he got the less people wanted to buy his house that was storing up all that anger from not being wanted by anyone. So having the goal of a starter home is like . . . you can't do anything in life or to the world if your original intent is not to actually do the thing but to do better than the thing.

ISAAC: So you're giving up on it?

PAIGE: It wasn't working. Let it go. Make the leap.

ISAAC: We live here. That makes it a home-home. You take care of it. Everyone is always trying to get out! The war doesn't work, just get out. The neighborhood doesn't work, just get out. We never commit.

[*A rage*] WE ARE NOT SELLING THIS HOUSE. END OF CONVERSATION!

[*Pause as everyone recovers from* ISAAC's *fit.*]

ARNOLD: Err.

[*Slight pause.* ISAAC *starts picking things up.*]

PAIGE [*to* ISAAC, *meaning the fit*]: Stop acting like your father.

[ISAAC *stops.*]

Put that down.

[ISAAC *puts it down.*]

Throw some water on your face. Max, put on a clean shirt and let's go.

[*Standoff.*]

ISAAC: I'll stay with Dad.

ARNOLD [*a little moan*]: Err.

PAIGE: No no no no no no no!

ISAAC: Someone has to stay with him. You go.

PAIGE: We're taking you with us.

ISAAC: I'll go next Saturday.

PAIGE: But next Saturday it will be an entirely different exhibit.

ISAAC: I can skip one.

PAIGE [*trying to entice*]: They're putting part of Saint Teresa on display. She's a dead body. You don't want to miss it, I.

[MAX *swats* PAIGE *to get her to be quiet.*]

What?

MAX [*whispering and gesturing to* ISAAC]: Body parts.

ISAAC: I'm not scared of body parts.

PAIGE [*to* MAX]: See.

ISAAC: Doesn't mean I want to go to a museum.

PAIGE: *Max* wants to go.

ISAAC: We don't do museums.

PAIGE: You don't know what we do.

ISAAC: Dad and I don't do museums.

PAIGE: Oh god no. We wouldn't want to expose you to culture.

MAX: We should stay. *I* just got here.

PAIGE: You wanted to go. You've been talking about going all week.

MAX: And now I don't.

PAIGE: We're going! We'll give Arnie a sleeping pill. I'll not let this
family get eaten alive by his atrophy.

ISAAC: It's not the kind of thing we like.

PAIGE: We love art.

ISAAC: We've never liked art.

PAIGE: We went to Paris when your dad was in the hospital and we
loved it.

ISAAC: You went on vacation when he was in the hospital?

ARNOLD [*a little moan*]: Err.

MAX: I always have comfort issues in museums anyway.

PAIGE: No you don't.

MAX: In Paris, in the Louvre, my feet hurt.

PAIGE: It was just the mones. They make you restless.

MAX: Don't tell me what my mones do to me. I wasn't restless, I was . . .
my feet hurt. 'Cause there's, like, hundreds of old paintings full of
. . . people pointing. And, it's fucking boring.

PAIGE: Max!

MAX: And everywhere you look all you see are paintings of horrible deaths and heads on platters, and arrows sticking out of naked bodies. But it doesn't engage you 'cause it's not what you must have seen in Afghanistan, but more, some dumb artist's promotion of it, you know?

ISAAC: No.

MAX: Like it's gross but more vicious than gross.

PAIGE: Art can't be gross, honey.

MAX: It's not art. It's propaganda.

PAIGE: ?

MAX: The real story has been erased or ignored and all that's left is someone's agenda, so it's boring and cruel at the same time and so eventually, when you look at it, all you can think about is how your feet hurt, or your back, or that it's a chore—

PAIGE: You can't tell me you think about your feet when you look at the Mona Lisa.

MAX: No, I like that one.

PAIGE: See.

MAX: Because the Mona Lisa is transgender.

ISAAC: That is not true.

MAX: It's a self-portrait of da Vinci.

PAIGE: Honey, I think Isaac might be right about this one.

MAX: Other people besides me say this.

ISAAC: That doesn't make it true.

MAX: Lots of people. Scholar people.

PAIGE [*believing it must be true then*]: Oh, okay then.

ISAAC: But it's all just their . . . what, their . . .

PAIGE: Use your words, Isaac.

ISAAC: It's just their . . .

MAX: Conjecture?

ISAAC: . . . Sure.

MAX: History is conjecture so why can't *hirstory* be the same thing?

PAIGE: Hirstory?

ISAAC: Oh Jesus Christ.

MAX: It's a word.

PAIGE [*trying the word out*]: *Hirstory!*

ISAAC: I don't know what that is but *history* is about proof.

MAX: I'm proof and conjecture. We're all proof and conjecture. So is da
    Vinci, who was trans but ze would have been killed if ze let people
    know, so ze did a self-portrait of hirself, changed hir name from
    Leonardo to Lisa and that's why ze's smiling.

[*Slight pause.*]

PAIGE: Well that settles it. Cultural outing day commences.

ISAAC: I'll stay and look after Dad.

PAIGE: No no no.

ISAAC: I'll get dinner ready.

PAIGE: We'll order delivery.

ISAAC: I wanna make dinner.

PAIGE: *Wanna!*

ISAAC: I want to make dinner.

PAIGE: It'll be more fun if you come.

ISAAC: Mama, I just got here. Between the house and Dad and Max and the Mona Lisa and hirstory . . . I'm a little tired. I'd like to stay. Okay? For me?

[*A slight pause.*]

PAIGE [*a little desperate*]: You can sleep in the car.

ISAAC: Mama.

[*A slightly longer pause.*]

PAIGE [*a deal*]: You catch up on sleep. Get adjusted. We'll go next Saturday. All three of us.

ISAAC [*not meaning it*]: Fine.

PAIGE [*getting ready to leave*]: Max, I am cooling down the car and then we are going.

[PAIGE *touches* ISAAC's *face, in a motherly way. He flinches a little.*]

[*With actual concern*] Sometimes you spend an entire lifetime preparing for something to be one way and right from the start it's another.

ISAAC [*not really understanding her*]: I guess.

[*A pause.*]

PAIGE: Don't care for him. Make him drink his shaky-shake, do the minimum and let him sleep. It's all he deserves. He has not earned the right to be cared for. Max, replace that wife-abuser shirt. I am cooling down the car, and then we are going.

[MAX *goes to hir bedroom to change hir shirt.*]

And honey, join the military, be promiscuous, and get an addiction to under-the-counter cleaning products, but when you are in this house, you will not use those products to clean. Understood?

ISAAC: Sure.

PAIGE: No, Isaac. I mean absolutely no cleaning. Deal?

ISAAC: Yeah.

[PAIGE *exits. There is a moment.* ISAAC *finds the Crisco and a rag and starts cleaning* ARNOLD'*s face thoroughly during the following scene.*]

MAX [*entering*]: If you want to get on the Internet you can use my computer.

ISAAC: Cool.

MAX [*getting hir laptop*]: I cleared the hirstory on it so you can't see how much porn I watch.

ISAAC: Thanks.

MAX: Paige thinks I jerk off all the time because I'm on hormones but it's just 'cause I'm a teenager.

[ISAAC *isn't paying attention to* MAX.]

Or maybe it's both. I don't know.

[ISAAC's *still not paying attention to hir.*]

It's weird not knowing. But kind of cool.

[ISAAC's *still not paying attention.*]

[*Getting in* ISAAC's *face to amuse him*] I mean, the horror and pleasure of the world is that it's usually both, right?

ISAAC: I don't really want to talk about your masturbation habits.

MAX [*disappointed*]: Okay. [*Slight pause*] The password for the computer is your name. [*Slight pause, then standing on a pile of clothes*]
And you have to stand up here to get the best reception 'cause we
have to pirate the neighbor's Wi-Fi.

ISAAC [*meaning, "that's pathetic"*]: Really?

MAX: I don't know. Shit gets expensive.

ISAAC: Dad doesn't get some kind of disability?

MAX: Paige didn't want to fill out the paperwork.

ISAAC: Jesus fucking hell.

MAX: She thinks that's what he gets for hating on socialism all the
time. Besides, we don't do financial responsibility anymore.

ISAAC: Well, that's gonna change.

MAX: When you get a job.

ISAAC: Yes.

MAX: Like last time.

ISAAC: I have experience now.

MAX: You were dishonorably discharged.

ISAAC: I can get something. '

MAX [*teasing*]: So you can spend your salary on drugs?

ISAAC: It's not that expensive.

MAX: I know.

ISAAC: What, you have a bunch of meth-head friends so you know everything?

MAX: I Googled it.

ISAAC [*an actual apology*]: Sorry.

MAX: I don't have friends. I mean I do, kinda, but, can you count people you've never met in person as friends? I mean, I guess I think you can, but people should be confronted with physicality as ritual before—

ISAAC: You should have friends. Actual friends.

MAX: It's not that easy.

ISAAC: Find a stranger, ask a question, listen to the answer, then ask a follow-up question.

MAX: That's a really problematic way of reducing the issue.

ISAAC: It's not that hard.

MAX: There is literally, not figuratively, but *literally* nobody in a hundred-mile radius that is like me.

ISAAC: I'm just saying—

MAX: I don't need you to protect me anymore.

[*Slight pause.*]

ISAAC: Okay?

[*Slight pause.*]

MAX: I talk to these guys on the Internet that live in a place called Wolf Creek. It's like a commune but for anarchist queers, so way cooler. It's a five-hour drive away but Paige won't let me go alone and it's not really the kind of place you want to go with your mother so—

ISAAC: You want me to take you?

MAX: Oh god no. Ha. I'm sorry. No. No. I just. No. Ha. No.

ISAAC: Okay!

MAX: I just mean, I don't think they'd appreciate me bringing my straight Marine brother. Or they would. But not for real reasons, more for, sexual-predator-humor reasons, or . . . I don't know.

ISAAC: It's fine.

MAX: I just mean, you'd mess up the safe space.

ISAAC: ?

MAX: The whole point is that it's a place made so people don't have to deal with things that are problematic.

ISAAC: I'm . . . problematic?

MAX: Yeah. You are. A little. It's not your fault. It's just, or maybe it is your fault but it's not really about you. [*Slight pause*] Are you mad at me?

ISAAC: I don't have to stay. I could just drop you off for a bit.

MAX: Really?

ISAAC: I guess.

MAX: I'm sorry. It's just, it's okay that you don't belong everywhere, right? I mean, the world is made for people like you.

ISAAC: If you say so.

[*Slight pause.*]

MAX: I don't know if I'm ready to go yet anyway. To Wolf Creek. I mean, I kinda can't wait. To go. I think about it all the time. But I'm not sure I have the skill set yet, you know?

ISAAC: No.

MAX: I mean, how can you belong somewhere if you've grown up in a place where you never belong. But, there is literally nobody here I'd even want to be friends with so—

ISAAC: I'm here.

MAX: It's kinda not the same thing.

ARNOLD: I'm. Wearing. Dress.

ISAAC: You made a sentence.

MAX: He talks more when Paige isn't around.

ISAAC: Is he a vegetable?

MAX: I dunno, more like an old person.

ARNOLD: Dress.

ISAAC: You want it off?

ARNOLD [*ambiguous about it*]: Emm?

ISAAC [*to* ARNOLD, *getting him to put his hands up so he can take his nightgown off and then putting a button-down flannel on him throughout the following scene*]: Up.

You really leave him here all day?

MAX: He just lies around.

ISAAC: It's not right.

MAX: She wants him to be humiliated.

ISAAC [*meaning, "you can't humiliate invalids"*]: He's an invalid.

MAX: She feeds him this mush so it gets all over his face and she won't wipe it off. It just hangs there. It gets all crusty. And he has to wear diapers. But she won't wash him properly. She makes him stand in the backyard and she hoses him down.

ISAAC: You can't let her do that.

MAX: Fuck him. It's called karma. Watch this.

[*To* ARNOLD] Arnold!

[MAX *points at* ARNOLD's *chest, like he has something on it,* ARNOLD *looks down, and* MAX *brings his finger up* ARNOLD's *face.*]

Arnold look.

[MAX *does it again and* ARNOLD *falls for it again.*]

Hey Arnold.

[MAX *does it again and* ARNOLD *falls for it yet again.*]

Arnie.

[*Again.*]

Hey.

[*Again.*]

Woohoo.

[*Again.*]

> [*Doing it over and over while ze says the following*] I could literally do this all day and he'll never—

ISAAC [*grabbing* MAX's *hand a bit more forcefully then necessary*]: Stop.

MAX: Ow.

[ISAAC *lets* MAX's *hand go and walks away from hir.*]

> [*Deflecting by changing the subject*] Your brain is exploding right now.

ISAAC: You should have written to say what was happening.

MAX: You didn't write me.

ISAAC: I don't do that kind of thing. You do that kind of thing and you didn't.

MAX: I'm allowed to be selfish 'cause I'm in transition.

ISAAC [*with regard to changing hir gender*]: She put you up to this.

MAX: Oh fuck off.

ISAAC: I just think she might have pressured you to change yourself in ways you might not be aware of.

MAX: I know what you think but that's just because Paige likes to appropriate my experience so it doesn't feel like it's my experience. She's not homeschooling me, I'm homeschooling her, and it's fucking exhausting. It's fucking exhausting teaching people.

PAIGE [*calling from outside*]: MAAAAAAAX!

MAX [*calling back*]: I AM TEACHING MY BROTHER!

[*To* ISAAC] Just . . . catch up. The world is going forward. There's no time to be worried about gender. Gender isn't radical. It's not even progressive. It's an everyday occurrence.

ISAAC: I barely recognize you.

MAX: I look the same, just hairy!

ISAAC [*laughing*]: That is so disgusting.

ARNOLD [*as if saying any random word, like "chair," or "dish," etc.*]: Sgusting.

[MAX *violently acts like ze is going to punch* ARNOLD. ARNOLD *cowers.*]

ISAAC: Hey!

MAX [*to* ARNOLD]: Idiot.

[*Slight pause*]

I better go.

ISAAC: I didn't puke 'cause of how you look.

MAX: Whatever.

ISAAC: I just throw up. Everybody vomits in Mortuary Affairs. It's what we get instead of medals.

PAIGE [*off-stage*]: MAAAAAAAAAAX.

[*Silence.*]

MAX: Gotta go. Paige wants to act like she's teaching me how to save the world. She's serious about not cleaning. Just so you know. I picked up a sock one time and she grounded me for a week.

ISAAC: It's not healthy.

MAX: Nothing new there. Now it just looks that way. [*Slight pause*]
You sure you don't wanna come?

[*A pause meaning no.*]

[MAX *starts to exit, makes a cartoon-like "you're-an-idiot" face at* AR-
NOLD. ARNOLD *flinches.* MAX *exits.* ISAAC *looks out the window. The car
drives off.* ISAAC *looks at the kitchen.*]

[*A long pause as* ISAAC *looks at* ARNOLD *and* ARNOLD *looks away.* AR-
NOLD *shivers.* ISAAC *turns the air-conditioning off and looks down at
his hands, which have makeup all over them.*]

ISAAC [*to* ARNOLD]: You're all over me.

ARNOLD: Don't. Like. Her.

ISAAC: Max?

ARNOLD: Err.

ISAAC: Mom?

ARNOLD [*an affirmation*]: Huh.

ISAAC: Paige. You know her name. You can say it. Paige. One after another after another.

ARNOLD: Another.

ISAAC: Yeah.

ARNOLD: Tired.

ISAAC: Drink your shake and you can go to bed.

[ARNOLD *doesn't drink the shake. Instead he holds his penis.*]

You don't want the shake?

ARNOLD: I'm cold.

[ISAAC *takes the shake from* ARNOLD. *Considers.* ISAAC *dumps the shake in the sink.*]

ISAAC: Okay?

ARNOLD [*meaning yes*]: Hm-hmm.

ISAAC: You look better now. More like how you're supposed to look.

ARNOLD: How?

ISAAC: Determined.

ARNOLD: TV.

ISAAC: Yeah, you like your TV. You sit in your easy chair, watch your TV, and you're easy. And then you get angry for being too easy.

ARNOLD: Angry?

ISAAC: You're a man. You're stern. You get red faced. You beat the dog with a bat for barking too loud.

ARNOLD: I don't like. Barking.

ISAAC: No, you don't.

ARNOLD: And?

ISAAC: You take a salt shaker with you everywhere.

[ARNOLD *picks up the salt shaker.*]

You eat hard-boiled eggs in the shower. I don't know why you do that.

ARNOLD: Because.

ISAAC: Right. You sit at the table with your shirt off and scratch your back with your dinner fork.

ARNOLD: And?

ISAAC: People like you. Enough. But not too much. Not enough to borrow things from you or send you invites.

ARNOLD: And?

ISAAC: And you take up space. You sweat. You leave your mark. Yellow stains on everything white. Under your pits, around your collar, on the toilet seat. You dole out allowances and punishments. You give me, you give Mom, us, bruises, welts when we do things or when we're too loud. You break our fingers if we leave a dirty dish in the sink.

ARNOLD: She. Talks. Too much.

ISAAC: She always talks too much.

ARNOLD: I don't like it.

ISAAC: You flick her with your finger to get her to stop.

ARNOLD: Like this.

[ARNOLD *flicks* ISAAC.]

ISAAC: Yes. She hates that.

ARNOLD: She takes it.

ISAAC: She asks you not to but you do it anyway because even though you're a man you want to be a child.

ARNOLD: You're a child.

ISAAC: I'm your boy grown up.

ARNOLD: What else?

ISAAC: You take me to batting practice and out driving but won't teach me how to do either. You sit and stare at things. I sit with you. We're quiet. You stare at things and I stare at you staring at the things.

ARNOLD: Things?

ISAAC: Lawns. Vinyl. Siding.

ARNOLD: Flowers? Stars?

ISAAC: No. Things. *Real* things.

ARNOLD: More.

ISAAC: You never cook except once a month when we eat fried chicken.

ARNOLD [*meaning, "I like chicken."*]: Chicken.

ISAAC: You take out the trash and obsess over shingles and yard work so you can be outside. You're fit but not so much it upstages you. You have a stash of porn in the garage and a secret jar of Polaroids, old flings who posed naked for you.

[ARNOLD *gets the Polaroids from a cookie jar.*]

You catch me staring at them and don't say anything, just leave. You like your beer to the point where you fight for it and whiskey to the point where you can't.

ARNOLD: Pictures?

[ARNOLD *throws the Polaroids up in the air like confetti.*]

ISAAC: Jesus.

ARNOLD: I like . . . [*closing his eyes and pointing to a random picture*] That one.

ISAAC [*grossed out by his pick*]: Oh no, Dad, no.

ARNOLD [*defending his pick*]: I like it!

ISAAC: Okay!

ARNOLD [*getting more aggressive about his defense*]: Tube sock titties.

ISAAC: I'm not trying to stomp on your girl.

ARNOLD [*on the attack*]: I stomp you!

ISAAC [*retreating*]: Hey, hey, okay. [*Slight pause*] That shirt does you good.

ARNOLD [*holding his penis*]: My penis is my best friend.

ISAAC: Okay.

ARNOLD: Heartbeat in a penis. Move nonstop. Like lava lamp. [*Slight pause*] Home.

ISAAC: You're home.

ARNOLD [*meaning, "I don't like the house being messy"*]: Messy.

ISAAC: Yes. You're a man. You like to come home to order.

ARNOLD: Sleep.

ISAAC: Okay.

[ARNOLD *gets up and goes to his bed.* ISAAC *watches him. He looks around, takes a deep breath, and starts to clean. A curtain falls.*]

ACT 2

[*Six o'clock in the evening, same day. The curtain opens to reveal the kitchen, which is much cleaner than when we last saw it.* ARNOLD *watches television in the living room. It's a sports channel.* ISAAC *is cooking and doing the dishes at the same time. When he is over the stove, it seems as if he's trying to stop himself from puking. We hear the car pull up, and after a bit* MAX *enters from outside.*]

MAX [*entering*]: Did you mow the lawn—

[*Regarding the clean house*] WOOOAAA! OHAAAAA! WOOOOAAAAA! What happened?

ISAAC [*continuing to clean during the following*]: You should know a few things. I'll be putting you to work. I'll be needing you to dust properly. Underneath all the furniture, including the beds. Move things to get underneath them if you need to but do not go around them. You may think the current state of the house means there has been slippage in Dad's exactitude. You are mistaken. You will straighten, polish, and demand the dirt's obedience.

[*Handing hir a duster and explaining it to hir like a child*] It's used to dust.

MAX: Mom's just parking the car.

ISAAC [*handing hir some polish*]: When you're done with that use this product to polish.

MAX: She's gonna freak.

ISAAC: One job at a time. The living room.

MAX: I just got home.

ISAAC: ?

MAX: It was Cultural Saturday.

ISAAC: Your point?

MAX: I've been explaining art to Paige for the last twelve hours.

ISAAC: And I've been cleaning all day.

MAX: I just want to jerk off and be quiet.

ISAAC: Life is not the finishing of events. It is a continuation. Each day you do what needs to be done with the understanding that there is no end to the doing. You find pleasure in the doing or you live in a tornado. You like living in a tornado?

MAX: Paige likes it.

ISAAC: What do you like?

MAX: I like to jerk off and be quiet.

ISAAC: You need to decide what kind of zee you're going to be.

MAX: Ze.

ISAAC: What kind of *ze* you're going to be. The kind who expects special treatment because ze's not really a man, or the kind who owns up to his, hir responsibilities and does hir job.

PAIGE [*from outside*]: Helllllooooooo!

ISAAC [*handing hir the duster again*]: The living room. You don't complain. You suck it up, drive on, and you clean.

[MAX *goes to dust the living room.*]

PAIGE: Hello! I'm hooooooome. Helloooooo! You have to talk back to me when I call out or [*coming in*] I can't get a sense of what I'm saying and I wonder if I exist.

[*A gut wrenching scream, from seeing the clean house, as if it were on fire*]

AHHHHHHHHHHHHHHHHH!

ISAAC: What's wrong?

PAIGE: What did you do?

ISAAC: I cleaned.

PAIGE: I told you I didn't want . . . why is the kitchen table in the kitchen?

ISAAC: That's where it goes.

PAIGE: I can't breathe with that normative table in here. What is that smell?

ISAAC: I'm making dinner.

PAIGE: We don't do chicken in this house.

ISAAC: Dad likes chicken.

PAIGE: He can't have wheat.

ISAAC: What?

PAIGE: We're celiacs.

ISAAC: What?

PAIGE: We're allergic to gluten.

ISAAC: No you're not.

PAIGE: You don't know what we are.

ISAAC: It's chicken.

PAIGE: Chicken rolled in gluten and fried.

ISAAC: It's what I've prepared.

PAIGE: It smells like the past. It's boiling in here. Is the air working?

ISAAC: I turned it off.

PAIGE: Why would you do that?

ISAAC: It's how I like it.

PAIGE: It's how your father likes it.

ISAAC: And how I like it and how Max likes it.

PAIGE: It's how your father likes it, so it's how you like it.

ISAAC: Yes.

PAIGE [*calling to the living room*]: ARNOOOOOOLD! Turn on the air-conditioning.

[ARNOLD *walks in and immediately begins eating chicken.*]

   [*Looking at* ARNOLD'*s shirt*] What are you wearing?

ISAAC: Clothes.

PAIGE: I don't want him in that.

ISAAC: He doesn't want to wear the pajamas.

PAIGE: The *nightgown* comes off and on easy.

ISAAC: You can get him out of a *shirt*.

PAIGE: The *nightgown* is easier to clean when he makes a mess.

ISAAC: You can wash a *shirt*.

PAIGE: You can't wash plaid. It's its own kind of filth. [*Slight pause*] It's a statement saying, I want you to know I care about not caring. Arnie, put on your nightgown.

ISAAC: Sit down, Dad.

PAIGE: Arnie, put on the nightgown.

ISAAC: Dad, sit down.

PAIGE: The nightgown.

[*During the following,* MAX *sneaks into the kitchen.*]

ISAAC [*simultaneous with* PAIGE'*s line below*]: It's okay, Dad, you don't have to. Don't leave. Forget the nightgown, Dad. Don't you take that shirt off. You stay right there. Stay right there and eat your chicken.

PAIGE: Put the nightgown on. Arnie, go put on your nightgown. Where's the nightgown? Arnie, take off that shirt and go find the nightgown. The nightgown.

MAX: I got it!

ISAAC [*simultaneous with* PAIGE'*s line below, to* MAX]: NO YOU DON'T!

PAIGE [*to* MAX]: HE WILL DO IT!

MAX: Okay!

[MAX *goes back to the living room.*]

ISAAC [*simultaneous with* PAIGE's *line below*]: Dad. Listen to me. Don't you go looking for that nightgown. You sit back down and wear your plaid. Dad. Dad. Dad. DAD!

PAIGE: The nightgown. Go find it. Find it. Find the nightgown. The nightgown. The! Night! Gown! The! Night! Gown! The! Night! ENOUGH!

[*With a vicious quiet determination*] Find the nightgown.

[ARNOLD *goes to get the nightgown.*]

[*Blaming* ISAAC *for* ARNOLD's *indecisive behavior*] Did you give him his shaky-shake?

ISAAC [*lying and not looking at her*]: Yeah.

PAIGE: You don't look at me when you talk to me?

[*A pause as* ISAAC *does not look at* PAIGE. *During the following,* PAIGE *throws out the chicken one piece at a time.*]

Did you have fun with your father today, cleaning when you specifically said you wouldn't?

ISAAC: We talked.

PAIGE: He never talks.

ISAAC: Because he's never been able to get a word in edgewise.

PAIGE: Don't you try to rein me in.

ISAAC: You're . . . emasculating him.

PAIGE: Is it that obvious?

ISAAC: He doesn't know who he is when you're around.

PAIGE: He knows who he has become.

[*Calling to* ARNOLD] ARNIE, MAKE EVERYONE A DRINKY-POO!

ARNOLD [*entering in his diaper and trying to pull on the nightgown*]: Drinky-poo.

ISAAC: Max can do it.

PAIGE: Let your father do it.

ISAAC [*calling to* MAX]: MAAAAAAAX, MOM WANTS YOU TO MAKE EVERYONE A DRINK!

PAIGE [*calling to* MAX]: ARNOLD WILL DO IT, HONEY. IT'S GOOD FOR HIM TO HAVE CHORES. Arnold, everyone gets some bubble.

ARNOLD: Bubble.

MAX [*entering with the duster*]: Should I stay or go?

ISAAC: I don't want a drink.

PAIGE: Because you've already dipped into your drug of choice?

ISAAC [*caught and not a good liar*]: What? I didn't . . . what?

[*Slight pause.*]

PAIGE: It's just bubble anyway. We don't do alcohol in this house anymore. We are not numbing ourselves. We are conscious beings. Arnold, get everyone some bubble.

ARNOLD: Bubble.

ISAAC: Tap water is fine.

PAIGE: Let him get you a little bubble.

ISAAC: No.

ARNOLD: Bubble.

PAIGE: Put a lime in it, Arnie.

ISAAC: No thanks.

PAIGE: It's like having a cocktail when you have a lime in it.

ISAAC: I'LL JUST TAKE WATER!

[*A pause.*]

PAIGE [*to* ISAAC]: You want a swizzle stick?

ARNOLD [*holding his penis*]: Swizzle.

PAIGE [*to* ARNOLD, *spraying him*]: Penis.

ISAAC: How 'bout you don't spray him like that?

PAIGE: Are you taking his side?

ISAAC: YES!

PAIGE: WELL!

[*Silence.* ARNOLD *holds his penis and gives* PAIGE *a seltzer water.*]

> Everyone, excuse me everyone! I have something I'd like to say to you all. I realize, if you met me today you would not like me, but because you did not meet me today, but many years ago at your inception, aside from you Arnie, but empathize with me here, okay?

ARNOLD: Okay.

PAIGE: Because you did not meet me today but many years ago, now you feel an obligation to like me. Believe it or not, *I*, if I had only met you today, the truth of the situation is, I would not want to spend time with you. But luckily for me this is not the case. What I am saying is, [*actual concern*] I have missed you and been afraid for you and I am glad you are with us.

[*Hearing the television for the first time*] Why is the television on?

ISAAC: Dad likes it.

PAIGE [*turning the television off*]: We don't do TV in this house.

ISAAC: All we do is TV.

PAIGE: Not since your father's stroke. Now we have family time where we do crafts and tell stories and play music and dress-up and do therapeutic shadow puppetry, but we don't do TV. And when we do do TV, we don't turn the volume on.

ISAAC: ?

PAIGE: It's easier to see what's *really* happening in the world with the volume off. That there is more beauty than despair.

ISAAC: If you'd been in a war you wouldn't believe that.

MAX: I don't believe that.

PAIGE [*to* MAX]: You're the one who told it to me.

MAX: It's sentimental and denies the range of actual experience.

PAIGE: Because an appreciation of beauty doesn't go with the brooding masculinity you've decided to take on since your brother arrived?

MAX: I'm not brooding.

[MAX *goes to the living room, with the duster, brooding.*]

PAIGE: ARNOOOLD! Away from the door. Yes. The door.

[*Going to make the shake*] Someone didn't make Arnold drink his shaky-shake.

ISAAC: MAAAAAAAAAX! I need you to polish the table.

MAX [*coming into the kitchen*]: I just started dusting again.

ISAAC: No complaining. Just do.

PAIGE: No, Max, let's have a salon, go get your banjo.

MAX [*a whine*]: Don't make me do that.

PAIGE: I want to show you off. Max plays the banjo now. Ze is filling our world with musicality. Get your banjo!

[MAX *goes into the living room as* ARNOLD *comes into the kitchen. When they pass each other* MAX *acts like ze is about to punch* ARNOLD *and* ARNOLD *flinches.* PAIGE *turns on the blender.* ISAAC *tries to keep it together.* PAIGE *eyeballs him, seeing if the blender noise is upsetting him. It is, but he doesn't puke. Instead he tries to steady himself, so he won't puke, during the following. It's difficult.*]

[*Handing* ARNOLD *the blender to drink from*] Drink.

[MAX *enters the kitchen with hir banjo, and while* PAIGE *is distracted,* ARNOLD *hides the blender without drinking the shake.*]

MAX: I just started.

PAIGE: You're getting good.

[*To* ISAAC] We're preparing a talent to offer the world for when we venture out.

MAX: I'm not getting good.

ISAAC: I wanna hear.

MAX: You don't.

ISAAC: Homes should have music.

PAIGE: Your *father* never liked music.

ISAAC: He wasn't always right.

MAX [*meaning the banjo*]: It's probably not for me.

PAIGE: Don't say that.

MAX: I only started 'cause I thought it was cool.

ISAAC: And because chicks dig banjos, right?

[*A slight awkward pause.*]

PAIGE: Max, did you see what Isaac did there? He tried to bond with you about chicks, as a way to say your sexuality is okay with him.

ISAAC: I am trying.

PAIGE: There's only one problem.

MAX: I'm a fag.

PAIGE: I hate it when you say that.

MAX: I'm attracted to guys.

ISAAC: I thought—

MAX: I know what you thought—

PAIGE: Max likes boys. And not just any boys but stinky hippie hairy gay boys ze stalks on the Internet. It's fantastic.

MAX: They're not hippies. They're anarchists.

PAIGE: They support themselves by selling rope sandals.

MAX: You don't know.

ISAAC [*to the universe*]: WHY DON'T I EVER UNDERSTAND ANYTHING?

PAIGE: And it's true you originally got the banjo because you thought it would give you access to the stinky hippie hairy gay sect, but now you're getting very good.

MAX: I suck.

ISAAC AND PAIGE: Don't say that.

MAX [*a defense*]: Okay!

[MAX *starts to play the banjo. Ze is not very good. Ze keeps messing up.* ISAAC, *who has been holding in his puke from the blender noise, suddenly can't hold it in any longer and pukes.*]

He just puked because of how bad I play.

ISAAC: I didn't.

PAIGE: Start again.

MAX: It makes him puke.

ISAAC: It didn't. I swear. [*Genuine*] It's just too awesome. I puked because it's too awesome.

[*An awkward pause.*]

ISAAC: Start again.

[MAX *starts again. Ze messes up a bunch.*]

MAX: Fuck.

PAIGE: Language.

ARNOLD: Fuck.

[PAIGE *sprays* ARNOLD.]

MAX: I'm not supposed to play the fourth string. I'm supposed to skip it every other time.

ARNOLD: Skip it.

PAIGE: You won't do it right, if you're riled up.

ISAAC: Slow it down and work it out, bit by bit.

PAIGE: It's because you're so empathetic.

ARNOLD: Skip it.

MAX: What?

PAIGE: You feel sorry for the string because it's getting left out of the song, so you always play it.

MAX: I do not.

PAIGE: You have to hate that string.

ARNOLD: Hate it.

MAX: I don't feel sorry for it.

PAIGE: If you hate it, then you won't play it.

ARNOLD: Hate it.

MAX: I can't hate it. I have to play it later.

ISAAC: Then just hate it for a little bit and then make up with it.

MAX: It goes by too fast. I have to play it two seconds later.

ARNOLD: Later.

MAX: I can't hate it and then make up in two seconds.

PAIGE: Slow it down and when you get it, speed it up.

ARNOLD: Up.

MAX: I don't want to hate it.

PAIGE: It's a string.

ARNOLD: Hate it.

MAX: I know.

PAIGE: It doesn't feel anything.

MAX: I know.

PAIGE: How is it my offspring care so much for inanimate objects?

MAX: It's not inanimate.

PAIGE: I blame you, Arnie.

ARNOLD: Inanimate.

MAX: It moves. It's not inanimate.

ARNOLD: Inanimate.

ISAAC: Try it again. Jesus Christ, Max.

PAIGE: Don't boss.

MAX: Forget it. I'm not playing it. I don't feel sorry for the string. I want to fuck it.

[*Pause.*]

PAIGE: What?

ARNOLD: Fuck it.

[PAIGE *sprays* ARNOLD.]

MAX: I want to fuck the string.

PAIGE: It's the mones.

MAX: Forget it.

PAIGE [*to* ISAAC, *a tongue twister*]: Hir's horny on hormones.

MAX: IT'S NOT THE MONES! I want to do what real musicians do when they play their instruments so good it's like they're fucking it.

PAIGE: You mean making love to it.

MAX: Don't neuter it. I want to fuck it. I want it to sweat and get embarrassed and have to change. And I can't do that with a banjo.

[*Taking the banjo back to hir room*] It's not my thing. People should do their thing. I tried it, it's not for me. I'll polish the stupid table.

[MAX *slams hir bedroom door.*]

PAIGE [*calling to* MAX]: You're going to be a visual artist anyway.

MAX [*coming back in and polishing the table*]: I'm not going to be a visual artist.

PAIGE: I see how you react when we go on Cultural Saturday—oh! The museum!

[*To* ISAAC] You should have come with us, I.

[*Knocking over a pile of folded laundry*] It was massive.

ISAAC: Hey!

PAIGE [*knocking over another pile while speaking to* MAX]: Life altering, wasn't it?

ISAAC: Stop.

MAX: Sure.

PAIGE: Don't you "sure" me. You loved it.

MAX: You're exaggerating my reaction to validate your experience.

PAIGE: You told me you loved it. The magnificent Saint Teresa body parts.

[MAX *swats* PAIGE *because she brought up the body parts again.*]

> If you hit your mother one more time I will immediately go to your room and flush your entire stash of testosterone down the toilet. Am I clear?

MAX [*actually sorry*]: Sorry.

PAIGE: The theme of the exhibit was about [*pulling out the brochure from her purse and reading*] "Partiality Meeting the Partial: An Examination of Engagement in Regards to the Damaged or Unfinished Work." So everything in the exhibit was missing something. Like the Saint Teresa body. Part of her was stolen so they only tour tidbits.

ISAAC: Sounds disrespectful.

PAIGE: It's exciting. Disrespectful were these *boys* who were at the museum.

MAX: They were just acting up.

PAIGE: Everywhere you go there are boys acting up. Shouting at each other, roughhousing next to art.

ISAAC: It's disrespectful.

PAIGE: Thank you. [*Genuinely happy about this*] Isaac, we agree.

ISAAC: Not the boys, the body.

PAIGE: Oh.

ISAAC: Someone dies, you put them to rest.

PAIGE: The saint doesn't mind, I. I mean, she *is* a martyr.

ISAAC: How we treat our dead is what—

PAIGE: Separates us from the blah blah? Everyone was happy yester-day and today everyone is a brooder. Why do you think that is, Isaac? Arnold, there isn't any ice in my drink.

ARNOLD: It's cold.

[ISAAC *grabs* PAIGE's *drink and puts ice in it. He gives it to her and then turns the air conditioner off.*]

PAIGE: Turn that air back on.

[ISAAC *doesn't move.* PAIGE *gets up and turns the air conditioner on.* ISAAC *turns it off.* PAIGE *turns it on.* ISAAC *goes to turn the air condi-tioner off.*]

DON'T YOU DARE.

[*A stand off.* ISAAC *goes into the living room, is about to punch a wall but stops himself.* ARNOLD *turns the air conditioner off.* PAIGE *turns it on.* ARNOLD *turns it off.* PAIGE *turns it on.* ARNOLD *flicks* PAIGE. PAIGE *slaps* ARNOLD's *hand as if he were a two-year-old.* ARNOLD *cries and goes back to his bed in the living room.*]

MAX: I don't want to be an artist. I want to live on a commune with a bunch of anarchists and make honey and be a gender-reassignment hirstorian.

PAIGE: What?

MAX: I want to gender-reassign hirstory. Convince people that da Vinci or Martha Washington or Queen Elizabeth were transsexual.

PAIGE: Is that a vocation?

MAX: The past got stolen and I want to steal it back!

PAIGE: You're not about the past, honey, you're about the future.

MAX: Don't tell me what I am.

PAIGE: Why are you acting so butch all of a sudden? Where did my sissy transman go?

[ISAAC *comes back to the kitchen with pent-up aggression.*]

MAX: I'm not a sissy.

ISAAC: Hell no, you're not!

PAIGE [*to* ISAAC]: You stay out of this!

MAX: I like sissies. I'm attracted to sissies. That doesn't mean I am a sissy.

PAIGE: You're a little sissy.

ISAAC: I don't think you're a sissy, Max.

MAX: Not that I couldn't be a sissy if I wanted to.

PAIGE: Then want to.

MAX: I'm trans-masculine.

ISAAC [*meaning, "Score one for Max!"*]: Oh!

PAIGE [*grossed out by* ISAAC'*s "dude" reaction*]: Eww. What is that, "Oh" thing?

ISAAC [*trying to get* MAX *to jump up and slap his palms that are held up*]: Up high. Up high.

PAIGE: Oh, don't you do that.

ISAAC: Do it, Max. Come on. Fucking do it.

[MAX *jumps up and slaps* ISAAC'*s palms.*]

[*Same as before but directed at* PAIGE] OH!

PAIGE [to MAX]: You're going to be ashamed of yourself in the morning.

MAX: Just because you don't want me to be trans-masculine doesn't mean I'm not trans-masculine.

PAIGE: It just seems like you're acting a little more trans-masculine today, since your brother arrived.

MAX: That's not true.

PAIGE [meaning, "whatever you say honey, but we all know that's not true"]: Okay.

MAX: Don't dismiss it like that.

PAIGE: Denying that you like art and stomping around about the past and anarchists and doing that rah-rah-I'm-a-winner-sports-slap thing you've always been appalled by but . . . [the same as above] Okay.

ISAAC: Max, help me make up the couch.

[MAX and ISAAC go to the living room.]

PAIGE: How about you stop bossing hir around?

ISAAC: How about you don't talk to me in that condescending tone?

PAIGE: Then stop behaving like a—

ISAAC: A man? We are men!

ARNOLD: Men.

ISAAC: THE MAKING OF THE BED MILITARY STYLE!

MAX: Cool.

PAIGE [to MAX]: Cool?

ARNOLD: Bed.

PAIGE: Since when do you believe anything to do with the military industrial complex is cool?

[ARNOLD *goes to the living room. During the following,* ISAAC *gives rapid fire, boot camp–like instructions to* MAX *and* ARNOLD *on how to make a bed, military style, but his diatribe is more for* PAIGE'S *benefit, to show how he is in charge of* MAX *and* ARNOLD. PAIGE *stays in the kitchen, where she decides to secretly set up the Shadow Puppetry Show.*]

ISAAC [*performed like a military tirade to new recruits*]: You will need one bottom sheet.

MAX [*holding up a fitted sheet*]: Got it.

ISAAC [*meaning, "say 'check,' instead of 'Got it'"*]: Check!

MAX [*as if to say, "Okay, don't get mad"*]: Check.

ARNOLD [*crowding* MAX]: Check.

MAX [*to* ARNOLD, *meaning "get out of the way"*]: Stop.

ISAAC: A top sheet.

MAX: Check.

ARNOLD: Check.

ISAAC: One pillow.

MAX: Check.

ISAAC: One pillowcase.

ARNOLD: Case.

MAX: Check.

[*To* ARNOLD] Move.

ISAAC: And one long-handled spoon.

MAX: Really?

ARNOLD [*going to get a spoon from the kitchen*]: Spoon.

ISAAC: You do not ask questions, you do!

MAX: Okay.

ISAAC: Step one! Tuck all of the edges of the sheet tightly and around the mattress.

MAX: We don't have a mattress.

ISAAC: Then you make do with what you have, Max!

MAX: Okay.

ARNOLD [*returning with a spoon*]: Spoon.

[*During the following, ISAAC rambles on. He's more intent on having PAIGE hear him (without looking at her) than paying attention to whether MAX and ARNOLD are doing it right. They try to keep up but aren't that successful because ARNOLD undoes almost everything MAX does. It is essentially a bed-making lazzi. MAX, as the lazzi progresses, gets more and more frustrated with ARNOLD, to the point where ze is pushing ARNOLD and on the verge of violence with him.*]

ISAAC: Step two! Lay the top sheet down, with the top edge even with the top of the mattress.

MAX: Top sheet.

ISAAC: Place the edge of the sheet with the longer hem, about two inches wide, at the head of the bed. Step three.

MAX: Whoa!

ISAAC: Lift the bottom of the mattress with one hand and tuck the bottom of the sheet between the springs and your other hand. Use the spoon—

ARNOLD [*taking the spoon from* MAX]: Spoon.

MAX [*taking it back from* ARNOLD]: Stop it.

ISAAC: —to tightly tuck the sheet. Step four! Lift the top sheet about a foot away from the foot of the bed. Pull straight up to form a diagonal fold.

ARNOLD: Fold.

MAX [*to* ARNOLD]: You're messing it up.

ISAAC [*overlapping them*]: And lay the fold flat on the top of the bed. Step five! Tuck the piece that is hanging from the corner under the mattress.

ARNOLD: Fold.

ISAAC: Step six!—

MAX: How many steps are there?—

ISAAC: Tuck the side of the top sheet securely under the edge of the bed. Fold the top side of the sheet down to form a nice crisp edge. Step seven!

MAX: Jesus.

ISAAC: Center your pillow at the head of the bed and look forward to a good night's sleep.

MAX: Forget it. You can't do anything in this fucking house.

[MAX *acts like ze is about to punch* ARNOLD. ARNOLD *flinches.* ISAAC *grabs* MAX *and pushes hir against the wall and holds hir throat with one hand, while acting like he's going to punch* MAX *with the other. This is a violent action and we should be scared.*]

ISAAC: Stop treating him like that!

MAX: Sorry.

PAIGE [*entering the living room and singing*]: *Shadow Puppetry Show!*

ARNOLD [*excited*]: Ooo!

[*During the following,* PAIGE *pulls up the sheets on the couch and begins dragging the couch pillows to the kitchen, to use them as audience seats.* MAX *retreats.*]

PAIGE [*to* MAX *and* ARNOLD, *sung*]: *A little help please.*

ISAAC: What are you doing?

PAIGE: We're going to do our shadow puppetry for you, I.

ISAAC: You keep taking my bed from me.

MAX [*an attack on* ISAAC]: Fun!

[MAX *and* ARNOLD *help her with the couch pillows.*]

PAIGE: I'll get the makeover kit.

   [*Calling from her bedroom*] WE'LL DO THE WHOLE FAMILY.

ISAAC: What? NO!

MAX [*an attack*]: It's fun.

ISAAC: DON'T COME IN HERE WITH THAT MAKEOVER KIT.

PAIGE [*from her bedroom, a demonic laugh*]: MWAH-HA-HA!

ISAAC [*to* MAX]: I thought you wanted to be a man.

MAX: A fag. I *am* a fag.

PAIGE [*from the bedroom*]: WE'LL DO OUR HAIR FIRST.

ISAAC: ABSOLUTELY NOT!

PAIGE [*throwing a wig from the bedroom into the kitchen*]: RAINBOW
FANTASY FOR MAX.

MAX: Score.

PAIGE [*throwing a Baby Jane wig in*]: BABY JANE FOR ARNOLD.

[ARNOLD *goes to pick up the wig.*]

ISAAC: Dad, you leave that wig there.

[ARNOLD *ignores* ISAAC.]

PAIGE [*throwing in a poufy pink wig for* ISAAC]: AND PINK POODLE
FOR ISAAC.

[*The massive pink and poufy poodle wig hits* ISAAC *in the face.* MAX,
who caught the makeup kit, starts putting makeup on hirself.]

ISAAC: You said you weren't a sissy.

MAX [*sing-songy*]: That was before she got the wigs out.

[ARNOLD *pulls a dress from a stack of clothes that* ISAAC *had folded,
knocking the stack over onto the floor in the process.*]

ISAAC: I JUST FOLDED THOSE!

MAX: I want the strawberry dress.

ARNOLD: Mine!

[ARNOLD *goes in the other room with the strawberry dress (and also snatches some makeup from* MAX). MAX *looks through the laundry for a dress during the following and puts one on.*]

PAIGE [*appearing at the entrance of the hallway, wearing a towering beauty pageant wig from the fifties*]: I used to have the worst hair. Giant. Frazzled monstrosity. And can you guess why? Because your father was having an affair with the family beautician.

ISAAC: Dolores Shadbolt?

MAX [*smearing lipstick all over hir face but talking about Dolores*]: Gross.

[ARNOLD *enters the kitchen wearing the Baby Jane wig, the dress, and fast and sloppy drag queen makeup.*]

ARNOLD: Dolores.

PAIGE: Story time! Dark and scary story time.

[MAX *turns off the lights.*]

ARNOLD [*speaking like a ghost*]: Oooooooo geeee booooo geeeee.

[PAIGE *turns a flashlight on (under her chin) and speaks the following as if in a nature documentary about dangerous creatures.* MAX *and* ARNOLD *make a vocal soundscape (the sound of a Polaroid, scissors, the murmur of girls gossiping, etc.) and hold up shadow puppets behind the sheet that tell the story of what* PAIGE *is saying. This is a rehearsed performance that, though amateur, they love doing.*]

PAIGE: Your father was having an affair with Dolores Shadbolt. I have the Polaroids to prove it. And the pictures of my atrocity called a hairstyle. Dolores's jealousy oozing out of every frontal flip. Of course I never knew. Although I should have suspected, walking around with all that ha-cha-cha up top. The vengeful mistress getting even with each little snip. I'd sit in her chair and tell her of my marital problems, and she'd snip away, goading me on. And when she'd finish with my style, I'd say, "I don't know, it seems a little much, don't you think?" but she just reassured me, got all those girls in the salon to do the same. I'd walk out, people would snicker. The whole world was in on it. But I kept on going to her. Confiding all my love secrets to the unknown nemesis wielding a curling iron and a bristle brush.

[MAX *and* ARNOLD *make demonic laughter sounds.* ISAAC *tears the sheet off and turns the lights on.*]

[*With no self-pity or sorrow, and making fun of the idiots who distinguish between "legitimate rape" and rape*] He also "legitimately" raped me. When I got my job and he lost his and he saw things weren't going his way, he "legitimately" raped me. And I shrugged. I think it was the shrug that gave him the stroke. His realization that even at his manliest, most desperate evil state, he was never going to be better than old hat. That's the man you want to care for?

ISAAC: I joined the Marines so I could learn how to stop him from doing things like that.

MAX: Really?

ISAAC: Maybe. But then I got there and . . . everyone was there because nobody knew how to stop whatever was happening at home. You can't leave places. The only useful job you can have in the places where everything is blown up is to care for the pieces.

PAIGE: Picking up those bodies has made you impartial.

ISAAC: What?

PAIGE: You have become an egalitarian empathizer.

MAX: That's a good thing.

PAIGE: To have empathy for some kid whose parents were blown to pieces by a fighter droid; that is a good thing. To have empathy for a man who hoards patriarchal privilege; that is bolstering his dominion. And we are not about shoring up [*indicating the house*] *this*. We're on a perpetual trip to bolster the new.

ISAAC: How are you paying for everything?

PAIGE: What?

ISAAC: Paris, and gas money to the city and your perpetual trip. If you can't afford Wi-Fi, how are you paying for everything?

PAIGE: Never you mind.

ISAAC: I do mind. I worry and I mind.

PAIGE: We don't worry about finances anymore. Financial worry is what your father does, did. We don't spend our whole lives planning and saving for trips we never go on. Right, Max? We go.

ISAAC: Well, I'll be here. So when you figure out you want to come home after you've done yourself in, there's a home to come home to.

PAIGE: No, Isaac, you won't.

ISAAC: He was awful, so what! Everything is awful. You honor what he was able to do and then you do better. At some point somebody has to stay home and do better.

PAIGE: Calm down.

ISAAC: I will not sleep in a box.

PAIGE: What?

ISAAC: All I've done for the last three years is care for blown-up limbs and intestines and pieces of brains. Half a heart. Knowing that if my body were to get blown to pieces, I'd want someone to care for them. To send them home. So I'm home. Despite what he made of it. I will not live in a box. I will not go crazy. That will not happen to me.

MAX: We sold the house.

ISAAC: ?

MAX: We sold the house to Rural Sprawl. That's how we've been paying for everything.

[ISAAC *rushes to the sink and pukes.*]

PAIGE: Jesus, I. You'd think there couldn't possibly be anything left.

[PAIGE *touches him on the shoulder to comfort him and he violently shrugs her off. Pause.*]

ISAAC: We have to get it back.

MAX: The money's gone.

PAIGE: We decided to improve ourselves instead of our house.

ISAAC: But we're still in it. If you sold it, why are we still in it?

MAX: It's like getting a reverse mortgage.

PAIGE: But better.

MAX: They let you live in it but they own it.

ISAAC: So we can stay here?

PAIGE: Until your father dies.

[*Pause.*]

ISAAC: Which you're hoping will be any day now.

[*Pause.*]

And when he does, where will we go?

PAIGE: With Max. To the future.

ISAAC: You think Max is going to provide the future for you?

PAIGE: Yes!

ISAAC [*to* MAX]: Are you going to do that?

MAX: I don't know. I don't care about houses. How are we supposed to care about things that have become burdens?

ISAAC: You just do.

PAIGE: Max and I don't do houses. We don't do things.

[*To* MAX] Right, honey?

MAX: I don't know.

PAIGE: You said nothing good came from things. Nothing good ever came from the middle class. [*Mocking*] "Ooooo I'm Middle Class. I'm Working Class. I deserve a home. I deserve."

MAX: I didn't say that.

ISAAC: How will you live? With your . . . cusp-of-the-new . . . hirstory shit-job?

MAX: Hirstory is not new. I'm not the new. I'm old. Just like everyone here.

PAIGE: Don't say that.

MAX: I don't want to be new. There is no new. How can you become new in a form that's so old its experimentation is a craft?

PAIGE: You blow it up! This property is on top of a landfill. If you go for a walk you'll see little pipes sticking out of the ground, releasing a giant buildup of gas created by the trash looming in the depths.

[*During the following,* PAIGE *goes to the wall and throws a picture off of it. A hole the size of a fist is behind it. She takes another picture off the wall and there is another hole. A third. Smashing the pictures to the ground. She rips an old decorative quilt off the wall and we see an indention where a body was thrown against it. She keeps pulling pictures and collectible plates down until the end of her speech.*]

He married me and built this because he thought we were things he could control. Cheap plywood and glue. This is the kind of house you can make a hole in from punching. That's not a house. It's him wanting to be more powerful than the home. Do we agree there is nothing to make from this? You want to be better? Go on a hunt for pipes, clog them up and applaud as your father's world explodes. Screw the Middle Class. WE ARE THE NEW. BEYOND GENDER. BEYOND POSSESSIONS. BEYOND THE PAST.

[ARNOLD *flicks* PAIGE.]

[*Pushing* ARNOLD *away*] Don't you do that to me.

[*He flicks her again.*]

You do that one more time, I swear to god I'll take you outside and spank you in front of all the neighbors.

[ARNOLD *takes his shake out from hiding and throws it on* PAIGE. *A beat.* PAIGE *grabs* ARNOLD *and starts spanking him violently.* ARNOLD *cries.*]

ISAAC: Stop it!

MAX: Mama!

[PAIGE *continues.* ARNOLD *tries to get away, but* PAIGE *begins to drag him to the door.* ISAAC *grabs her hand, spins her around, and punches her hard, in the face.* ARNOLD *retreats to a corner.*]

[ISAAC *exits. Returns with a bat. He begins to smash the air conditioner.* PAIGE *and* MAX *stare at* ISAAC *as he continues to smash it. It takes a long violent time. He finishes. He is exhausted. He begins to sob.*]

PAIGE [*matter-of-fact, through the rest of this scene*]: I need you to leave, Isaac.

ISAAC: Oh god.

MAX: It's okay.

ISAAC: I'm sorry.

MAX: It's okay.

PAIGE: I need you to leave.

ISAAC: Oh god.

MAX: No, Mama.

PAIGE: You are no longer welcome.

ISAAC: Oh god.

PAIGE: You are not welcome.

MAX: It's okay.

ISAAC: I'm sorry.

PAIGE: You are not listening. You are no longer welcome.

MAX: Don't say that.

PAIGE: Wipe your tears. Pull yourself together and listen to me. It's why we sent you, all the boys, to the wars to begin with. What do you do with leftover pieces? You can pretend you will use them for something but you never will. At a certain point you have to dispose of them.

MAX: Don't say that.

PAIGE: You are no longer necessary. For the rest of your life you will pick up useless pieces. Mourn your dead. Your death.

ISAAC: I'm sorry.

MAX: It's okay.

PAIGE: It's not okay, Max.

ISAAC: I don't have anywhere to go.

PAIGE: Go be on the street. Be with your brothers and your fathers and your ruined . . . possibilities, while the rest of us move on without you.

ISAAC [*sobbing*]: I want to be home—

PAIGE: You will never go anywhere but the places you have already been.

ISAAC: I want to go home.

PAIGE: But the places you've already been don't exist anymore.

ISAAC: Mama.

PAIGE: I would tell you to kill yourself here but I don't want to clean the mess.

[*Pause.* ISAAC *pulls himself together slightly. He gets his duffle bag from the living room and starts to leave. He stops. Looks at* MAX. MAX *doesn't know what to do.* ISAAC *leaves. Nobody moves. Eventually* MAX *goes to the window. A beat.*]

[*Looking at the disheveled place*] All we need now is a few dozen cats, don't you think? To finish setting the picture.

[*A slight pause*] Why didn't he come to the museum?

[*To* MAX] What are you doing over there, honey? We should get you some bubble. [*Getting hir some seltzer*] You'll be happy if you drink your bubble.

MAX: I can't see him.

PAIGE: When you're older, and I know that's annoying, when older people tell you you'll understand when you're older—

MAX: Just say it.

PAIGE: You lose things. Important things. And you can't get them back. And some of the things you say are lost, are actually gone.

MAX: He shouldn't have done that to you, but still you shouldn't have—

PAIGE: I have to choose, and I choose us.

MAX: I don't want to be here.

PAIGE: You don't have to be.

MAX: I don't wanna be here with any of this.

PAIGE: Good.

MAX: There are places where it's easier. Where people aren't like this.

PAIGE: Of course.

MAX: I don't want to be here with you.

PAIGE: I know.

MAX: It, you, it's all debris.

PAIGE: You'll get away. You'll do better.

[ARNOLD *moans and wets himself. His diaper leaks, and his urine makes a puddle.*]

MAX: Dad wet himself.

PAIGE: I know.

MAX: He wet himself.

PAIGE: Let it rot.

[MAX *looks at* ARNOLD. *After a bit, ze makes a decision and goes to him.*]

MAX [*getting him to gently raise his arms*]: Up.

[ARNOLD *puts his arms up and* MAX *takes his wet nightgown off (he wears a diaper underneath).* MAX *brushes* ARNOLD'*s hair down, calms him, and starts to clean up the urine with a nearby towel.*]

PAIGE: Leave it.

[MAX *cleans.* PAIGE *stifles a sob.*]